AGAPE

SHREESH
KAKKAR

INDIA • SINGAPORE • MALAYSIA

ISBN 979-8-89133-714-5

Contents

Look

Look into my eyes,

Look at me smiling like an idiot,

Waiting to tell you that I love you.

Written in the Stars

"Written in the stars,

Is the answer to who we are."

Endless

"Love for you as deep as the ocean,

As endless as the sky;

Love with the promise that our lives would not be dry,

We will still end up laughing even on the days we cry."

The Way

"It is the way you entered the room,

With a vibe of your own.

With a vibe that knocked off formality and awkwardness.

It is the way you spent your time,

Like you are in your own environment,

In your own comfort zone.

It is the way you look at me from across,

Making eye contact and smiling.

It is the way your eyes talk to me,

When your lips do not say a word;

Silent, yet so loud.

It is the way you came in,

Carved your way easily,

Through those high walls that keep people at a distance.

It is just the way you effortlessly did all these things."

Souls Like You

"Souls like you are hard to find,
Beautiful, sweet and the most kind,
Pretty inside-out,
The best without a doubt.

Souls like you are hard to find,
People who fail to appreciate you are blind,
This heart and mind, a combination so rare,
Not treating you right would not be fair.

Souls like you are hard to find,
Impossible to keep away from one's mind."

Pages

"I sit here filling pages,

And it feels like it's been ages,

But it's just been an hour,

And my pen has been showing its power.

I sit here searching for new songs,

And putting into two separate jars – the right and wrongs."

Who Sent You

"Who are you? Why are you here?

Is all this true or are you just completing a dare?

Of all the people, why have you chosen me?

What is it that you want from me?

The way you are and the way you care,

Makes me question, who are you and why are you here?

The way you are and the way you care,

Is hard to trust because it is so rare.

What is it that you do, but I do not see,

Why do you stick even when you know, you and I cannot be we?

I want my answers, I want to know you,

I want to know; I want to know who sent you."

Fire

"Are you fire or just a flame?
He replied,
It depends upon your game,
Upon the levels of flame, you can maintain,
Whether you can handle being the main,
Whether you can shower love in the rain?"

Mystery Room

"Every common space that I share with you,
Every room that I am in with you,
That is full of people, is a mystery room.

Waiting for you to look at me,
So, I can tell you that I love you,
Waiting for you to look at me,
So, you can see the smile on my face.
The smile that says I adore you."

Robbed

"Girl, it must be you again,
I know you have come to rob one more time,
Rob me of my lines,
Rob me of my senses,
To take my breath away, again.
Girl, it must be you again,
I know you have come to sweep me one more time,
Sweep me off my feet,
To make me fall in love with you, again."

Nowhere

"To nowhere,

But to you."

Lost Frequencies

"Looking for the right frequency on my life's radio,
I was able to tune into your channel,
Even though I was in the middle of nowhere,
What a lucky strike that.
Your channel gave me music for the rest of my ride,
It was necessary as I had nobody by my side.
Finding that right frequency made me happy,
I hope I never lose the signal,
Because without that I was lost.
Your channel served as an escape for me,
Escape from the land of lost frequencies."

Forecast

"Went online to check the weather forecast,

Report said it's raining, it's raining love,

Between the two of you, irrespective of your caste,

Breaking barriers and rising above,

Rising were the water levels with us,

Drowning, we were drowning in love.

Head over heels, making reels, cracking deals,

Experiencing all the feels.

Went online to check the weather forecast,

Report said the sun is out; the sun is here to bring warmth;

Warmth in her arms,

warmth when hand in hand you're running together through the sunflower farms."

Sunflower

"You are the bright yellow light in the sky,

That marks the beginning of the day.

Do not know if you are the sun or the flower,

But whatever you are, you have a lot of power.

Valuable and attractive just like a sunflower,

Also, an uncommon specie with the tendency to grow,

Vibrant, Strong and known for beauty,

You are such a cutie.

You are the bright yellow light in the life,

That marks the presence of positivity,

Representation of sunshine, happiness and hope,

You make life so dope."

Gold Mine

"You are gold, I would not say mine,
But to me, you are definitely a gold mine.
Precious! Ah, so damn fine,
To me, you are definitely a gold mine.
With depth as deep as the deepest ocean,
There is nothing but pure gold in every portion.
No matter what anyone would have told,
I know 'cause I recognise it is 24 karat gold.
You are gold, I would not say mine,
Precious! Ah, so damn fine."

Out of This World

"Is it you who is out of this world?
Or is it me who has stepped into your world?
Is it you who is the umbrella?
Or are we both standing under the same umbrella?

In this world or under this umbrella cover,
I am nothing more than a crazy lover,
Who would never miss a chance to write about you,
Just to let you know that I am crazy about you.

This question that I seek an answer to,
And wonder if you would believe, like I do,
That yes, of course, you are out of this world."

Library

"Your library is all about books;

And my library? It is all about you."

It be Like That

“The life keeps moving forward,

Keeps increasing its pace,

That is the time I take the foot off the pedal,

So that we can be together,

In the hope that you will hold my hand from behind,

Keep me with you,

My life's pace with yours'.

The life keeps moving forward,

And so do the people,

But I slow down,

Die a little, cry a little,

To live my life, to just be fine,

In the hope that you will catch me when I will be falling,

Save me like your favourite superhero,
Hold me like you will never let me go,
It be like that at times,
The life increases its pace,
But I slow down,
Die a little, cry a little, daily,
To be with you, just to be with you,
To not let you go far from my sight,
To keep you with me, always."

Skydive

"Would you jump from the wall?
The wall that you have built so high,
So high that no one can come close,
Come close to you so no one can hurt you,
Hurt you in ways that are beyond repair.

If I offer, would you hold my hand,
Hold my hand and trust me,
Trust me enough to jump from that wall,
From that wall to land in a new world.

A new world that I want to take you to,
Take you to, so you could experience new things,
New things that you have been blocking off,
Blocking off by staying behind your wall.

If I offer, would you jump with me?
Would you fight your fears?
Would you give the world another chance?
Would you let me love you?"

Vision

"My vision might not be a perfect 6/6,

But I can see my future with you.

My vision might not be a perfect 6/6

But I know if things go wrong, I will be ready to fix.

It takes not the perfect vision, but, the visionary in you,

The visionary who can see through,

Through the obstacles, through the blocks,

To win for your love, to win against the clock."

Secrets

"Let us get drunk, smoke a cigarette,

You tell me yours; I will tell you, my secrets.

Take my hand and let me walk with you,

Bare foot,

Over all your fears and insecurities,

For a good time lies ahead."

Butterflies

"I saw her and looked at my stomach,
Asked it to meet butterflies;
Said, this looks like all smiles and no cries,
Why not make a move and try.

Put the mathematics to work,
One plus one would make it eleven,
Kept calculating twenty-four seven,
Two plus two, would it be worth,
Is she the one for me on this Earth,
Three plus three, would it be WE,
Or another heartbreak, leaving only ME?"

Cards

"Do not play cards,

But guess I made the right moves,

Hit the jackpot,

Pulled the Queen.

Now hand in hand,

We are off the scene,

Away from the World black and white,

Moving on the Chess Board left and right,

Protecting my Queen with all my might."

I Wish

"I wish I could take your stress away,
Put all the mess away.
I wish I could hold your hand,
Help you take a stand.
I wish I could be on the other side,
Ride with you over every tide.
I wish I could say those words,
Give you the best of all the worlds."

Her

"Her eyes on food,

Mine on her,

Awestruck I stood.

Her eyes on food,

Mine on her,

Wondering how she always looks so good."

All the Places

"Of all the places I have seen,

Of all the spaces I have been,

I found peace in your arms.

In your arms, where the storms are calm,

The tides are low, away from the city chaos,

I feel my heart grow,

Grow even more fond of you."

Plans

"I would cancel all my plans,
If you tell me you want to see me,
I would not think twice,
To tell you that you look like the rest of my life.

I would cancel all my plans,
Just to steal that one glance.
If you tell me you want to see me,
You know I would be extremely happy.

I would cancel all my plans,
If you tell me you want to see me."

My World

"People watch the world with their eyes,
I have seen my world in those eyes.
People go around the world,
In those arms, I found my world.

People watch the world with their eyes,
I found mine in those nerves - cold as ice.
I got lucky when I rolled the dice,
There is nothing more I want from life."

Ours

"This wardrobe might be mine,

But the clothes are ours,

The clothes bought by me,

But worn by us.

This life might be mine,

But now, it is dedicated to you.

Dedicated to you in all aspects;

Promise for it to be full of love and respect."

Stars and the Moon

"To all the stars and the moon,
Take care of her till I come back home.
To all the stars and the moon,
To tell her I miss her, pop-up even in the noon.

To all the stars and the moon,
Do not let her life ever be dark,
To all the stars and the moon,
Tell her I will come back; I will come back soon.

To all the stars and the moon,
Shower happiness and love on her,
To all the stars and the moon,
Just tell her that she is loved by this cartoon."

Rest of Our Lives

"A poem, a book, a letter,
I want to write for you, write to you,
Today, tomorrow, and for the rest of our lives,
I want to pen it all down for you.
Lots of love, care and strength,
I wish for you, pray for you,
Today, tomorrow, and for the rest of our lives,
I want you to have it all."

Rightfully Yours

"Pick the gun and take the aim,
Pick the dart and throw at it,
You do not have to hesitate even a bit,
You have the right, so make your claim.
I surrendered a long time ago,
Surrendered myself to you.
So, tell me, if not you, then who?
Not sure if this is, but this might be a clue,
To tell you again, what you already know.

The things you ask for, and the things I get for you,
My heart and all of me,
Is for you to rightfully claim,
Claim like everything is rightfully yours."

Remedy

"When the mind is sick and negativity rains heavily,

Thinking about you works as a remedy,

A remedy no doctor could possibly ever give,

A remedy that gives positivity another chance to live.

When the heart is sick and it pumps negativity,

You are the calming positive melody,

A melody with magical healing power,

A melody like a summer blossoming flower."

Hundred

"Sachin goes for 99, yet again,

A run short of another hundred to add to his record.

This is not how it will end,

Broken hearts, frowning faces.

It will continue and lead to celebrations and firecrackers,

Fast - beating hearts and happy faces;

It will be a story that will inspire hundreds and make hundreds jealous."

All I Ask

"All I ask is for you to take a chance on me,
Bet on me,
Go all in,
Hoping you would win.

All I ask is for you to hold my hand,
Take a stand,
Forget what people would say,
Carve out your way.

All I ask is for you to walk by my side,
Be my guide,
Walk me to the finish line,
Where I call you mine.

All I ask is for you to take a chance on us,

Bet on us,

Go all in,

Hoping we would win."

Most Days

"On most days I wish you never see my unfinished drafts,

But on some days, I wish you would;

There are things, I wish I could say to you,

And things I wish you could.

On most days I wish you could see my craft,

But on some days, I wish you would not;

There are things I want to show to you,

And things I wish you would.

On most days I wish you would come to me,

On some, I wish you would not;

There is mess that makes my heart scream,

There is mess that makes my heart dream."

Hold My Hand

"Hold my hand, tight,
Together we will get through the fights,
Love, I promise we are going to be alright,
Just hold my hand, tight.
I will make sure the grip is strong,
And we continue for long,
Love, I promise I will not let it go wrong,
And as we walk, I will sing you a song.

Step by step together,
We will make it through every weather.

If you leave me, I know I will be lost,
I will not be able to get back to you at any cost.

Take me somewhere with you,

There I will start my life like new,

Where the struggles will be more and comforts few,

Where, if nothing, I will have you.

Where a world I will build,

For I believe I am skilled,

And I know I will be thrilled (to be there),

For it is you that the world is going to be filled with.

Love, I promise; Just hold my hand, tight. Will you?"

The Room

"Tonight, I went again,
Into the room in my heart,
The room where you and I created art.
Tonight, I went again,
Into the room in my heart,
The room where you and I have been
Living from the start.

Into the room I go,
Go when I'm feeling low,
Into the room I go,
Go when I feel a blow."

Fall

"If you leave my hand,
I will fall.
I will not die, but I will not be living either,
Because I will be too wounded,
Considering the height, I will be falling from."

Love

"If we do not make it,
For the rest of my life, I am going to fake it,
Fake it, for fake is what this world is.
It will tell you that love always wins,
But love is what fails the most,
Love is what gets blamed the most,
Ignites the flames the most.
It wins when it happens,
If not, they say it was not meant to be,
Trying to cover it up and protect you mentally."

Fictional

"Said she would like to stay single till she finds her own fictional man who would love her unconditionally,

Said she would like to stay single till she finds her own fictional man,

That made me go 'damn'

Made me wish I was fictional,

Hoping she would be my fan.

Said she would like to stay single till she finds her own fictional man,

Who would give her love, so unconditional,

Step into her jurisdiction,

Cause their love a friction.

Said she would like to stay single till she finds her own fictional man,

But tells me I am too good to be true,

Like straight out of the book, man."

When it Comes to You

"When it comes to you,
I tend to forget my lessons,
Those life lessons that I learnt the hard way,
Without anyone by my side.
Love, attachment, trust,
What builds a castle, what turns to dust,
Ego, anger, fight,
What breaks you, what keeps you up at night.

When it comes to you,
All my understanding goes for a toss,
I experience something we call a loss,
A loss of knowledge, calm and grip.
Song, writing, dance, art,

What expresses love, what tells you secrets of my heart,

Misunderstanding, communication gap,

What leads you in the wrong direction on the map."

Fingers

"Blocked you with the same fingers
That dreamt of being locked with yours,
That dreamt of running through your hair
While you lay with your head on my chest.

Blocked you with the same fingers
That used to text you all day,
Asking you to stay in my life,
For as long as you can."

Love You The Same

"I felt endless love for you inside me,
Even if you destroy the house or count on me,
I will still love you the same.
Love you even on the darkest nights,
And even in the loneliest moments,
I will still love you the same.
People will call me crazy,
And ask me to move on,
But I will still love you the same."

Never Met You

"I wonder what life would be,
If you were to be mine,
A dream come true, or just simply fine,
I wonder what life would be.

Would it be a fairy tale?
Like Cinderella's perfect shoe fit,
Like Yuvraj's 6 X 6 hit,
Would it be a fairy tale.

I wonder what life would be,
If you were to be mine,
But I also wonder what life would be,
If I never met you."

Parallel Universe

"In a parallel universe,
You would be sitting shotgun,
Hand in hand, hand on gear,
And on the backseat,
Our princess,
With her teddy bear."

Last Time

"And just like that, I wrote for the last time."

www.ingramcontent.com/pod-product-compliance
Lightning Source LLC
La Vergne TN
LVHW091235150826
845673LV00003B/1149

* 9 7 9 8 8 9 1 3 3 7 1 4 5 *